Westview Youth Group

PRAYER

An Adventure with God

12 Studies
for individuals or groups

David Healey

With Notes for Leaders

D1113054

INTERVARSITY PRESS
DOWNERS GROVE, ILLINOIS 60515

InterVarsity Press® is the book-publishing division of InterVarsity Christian Fellowship®, a student movement active on campus at hundreds of universities, colleges and schools of nursing in the United States of America, and a member movement of the International Fellowship of Evangelical Students. For information about local and regional activities, write Public Relations Dept., InterVarsity Christian Fellowship, 6400 Schroeder Rd., P.O. Box 7895, Madison, WI 53707-7895.

Cover photograph: Dennis Frates

ISBN 0-8308-1053-6

Printed in the United States of America ♾

15	14	13	12	11	10	9	8	7	6	5
05	04	03	02	01	00	99	98	97		

Contents

Getting the Most
from LifeGuide® Bible Studies

Many of us long to fill our minds and our lives with Scripture. We desire to be transformed by its message. LifeGuide® Bible Studies are designed to be an exciting and challenging way to do just that. They help us to be guided by God's Word in every area of life.

How They Work

LifeGuides have a number of distinctive features. Perhaps the most important is that they are *inductive* rather than *deductive*. In other words, they lead us to *discover* what the Bible says rather than simply *telling* us what it says.

They are also thought-provoking. They help us to think about the meaning of the passage so that we can truly understand what the author is saying. The questions require more than one-word answers.

The studies are personal. Questions expose us to the promises, assurances, exhortations and challenges of God's Word. They are designed to allow the Scriptures to renew our minds so that we can be transformed by the Spirit of God. This is the ultimate goal of all Bible study.

The studies are versatile. They are designed for student, neighborhood and church groups. They are also effective for individual study.

How They're Put Together

LifeGuides also have a distinctive format. Each study need take no more than forty-five minutes in a group setting or thirty minutes in personal study—unless you choose to take more time.

The studies can be used within a quarter system in a church and fit well in a semester or trimester system on a college campus. If a guide has more than thirteen studies, it is divided into two or occasionally three parts of approximately twelve studies each.

LifeGuides use a workbook format. Space is provided for writing answers to each question. This is ideal for personal study and allows group members to prepare in advance for the discussion.

The studies also contain leader's notes. They show how to lead a group discussion, provide additional background information on certain questions, give helpful tips on group dynamics and suggest ways to deal with problems which may arise during the discussion. With such helps, someone with little or no experience can lead an effective study.

Suggestions for Individual Study

1. As you begin each study, pray that God will help you to understand and apply the passage to your life.

2. Read and reread the assigned Bible passage to familiarize yourself with what the author is saying. In the case of book studies, you may want to read through the entire book prior to the first study. This will give you a helpful overview of its contents.

3. A good modern translation of the Bible, rather than the King James Version or a paraphrase, will give you the most help. The New International Version, the New American Standard Bible and the Revised Standard Version are all recommended. However, the questions in this guide are based on the New International Version.

4. Write your answers in the space provided in the study guide. This will help you to express your understanding of the passage clearly.

5. It might be good to have a Bible dictionary handy. Use it to look up any unfamiliar words, names or places.

Suggestions for Group Study

1. Come to the study prepared. Follow the suggestions for individual study mentioned above. You will find that careful preparation will greatly enrich your time spent in group discussion.

2. Be willing to participate in the discussion. The leader of your group will not be lecturing. Instead, he or she will be encouraging the members of the group to discuss what they have learned from the passage. The leader will be asking the questions that are found in this guide. Plan to share what God has taught you in your individual study.

3. Stick to the passage being studied. Your answers should be based on the verses which are the focus of the discussion and not on outside authorities such as commentaries or speakers. This guide deliberately avoids jumping from book to book or passage to passage. Each study focuses on only one

passage. Book studies are generally designed to lead you through the book in the order in which it was written. This will help you follow the author's argument.

4. Be sensitive to the other members of the group. Listen attentively when they share what they have learned. You may be surprised by their insights! Link what you say to the comments of others so the group stays on the topic. Also, be affirming whenever you can. This will encourage some of the more hesitant members of the group to participate.

5. Be careful not to dominate the discussion. We are sometimes so eager to share what we have learned that we leave too little opportunity for others to respond. By all means participate! But allow others to also.

6. Expect God to teach you through the passage being discussed and through the other members of the group. Pray that you will have an enjoyable and profitable time together.

7. If you are the discussion leader, you will find additional suggestions and helpful ideas for each study in the leader's notes. These are found at the back of the guide.

Introducing Prayer

I don't think it would take much research to discover that most Christians would say they find prayer hard. There are books and programs, prayer diaries and prayer conventions, but most of us know in our heart of hearts that we could pray more, or more sincerely, or less selfishly than we do now. Most writing and talks on prayer are about how to pray. But one of the most important things we can learn from the examples of prayer in the Bible is why we pray. This helps us to see the importance of prayer in our relationship with God, and in the outworking of his plans.

We learn about prayer in the Bible by seeing other people do it. John White, whose book *Daring to Draw Near* you will find referred to at various places in this LifeGuide, writes, "What we have lacked was the insight that comes from eavesdropping on some of the most significant prayers in human history" ([Downers Grove, Ill.: InterVarsity Press, 1977], p. 7).

The Variety of Prayer

One of the things you discover fastest when you look at the prayers of the Bible is the variety of prayer. Intercession—which is the principle focus of studies 1-6—happens in many different forms, with different effects. Thanksgiving and prayer in the face of conflict are recurrent themes in Psalms and Acts and the central focus of Hannah and Mary. Repentance, inevitable when men and women become intimate with a holy God, recurs regularly, particularly in the great prayers of Abraham, Moses, Daniel and Nehemiah. Prayer for our own needs, and the needs of others, is real, stark and honest in the prayers of Hannah and Paul.

Whatever form prayer takes, biblical prayers underline that prayer has at its heart two-way communication with God. It is where we talk to God and listen to him, discovering his purposes for the world and those around us—purposes always consistent with his revelation to us in Scripture. By praying we embark on an adventure to become more involved in the outworking of God's plans. In many cases those who prayed were also part of the way in which God answered their prayers. Nehemiah's prayer (study 3) commences with his concern about Jerusalem and ends with him asking for the resources to rebuild the city walls. Prayer is part of God involving us in his plans, and so is part of being remade in his likeness.

The Importance of Prayer

Evangelism should be one of our priorities. A vital part of evangelism is praying for others (intercession), yet this is often one of the weakest areas of our prayer lives. And Satan works hard to discourage us from praying. It is also easy for Satan to make us guilty about our prayerlessness. We are fed the lie that we have to be someone with a "ministry of prayer" before we ever pray beyond our own daily concerns.

The prayers we encounter in the Bible are about ordinary people being involved in God's purposes, despite weakness, fear and mixed motives. The Bible enables us to get alongside biblical characters, to understand a little of why they prayed and how they saw God. That can only encourage us. We expect great pray-ers to pray big, theologically worded prayers. Read aloud the prayers in some of the studies, and see how long they take you. Count the number of big words. You will be surprised how few there are. Prayer need not be complicated to be significant.

Several practical things need to be said about the studies:

☐ Each study has an idea at the end for you to apply what you have been learning to your prayer life. You will get the most out of these studies if you try these exercises in your own prayer life or with a group.

☐ I strongly recommend *Daring to Draw Near* as a good primer on the subject of prayer. It is suggested leader's background reading in several studies, but also contains helpful material on the other prayers of the characters featured in the studies. The background reading suggested in the leader's notes is also optional, but will help you deal with the questions the passage brings up.

☐ God knows that we find prayer tough. He forgives us for our failings and helps us to start afresh time and time again.

The adventure of prayer is for all of us to be involved in. Unlike some Hollywood adventures, it is high risk, high pain, long-term, hard work, unglamorous, and potentially very costly. It's also something we don't graduate out of. It's a lifelong adventure that begins where we are. Most of all it is an adventure hand in hand with the One who went to the cross for us and intercedes at the right hand of the Father for us. And who wants us in prayer to enter deeper into his purposes for the lives of those around us.

1
Conversing with God: Abraham

Genesis 18:16-33

If we are honest, many of us admit that we pray most often when we are faced with a crisis, such as exams, big career decisions, dealing with suffering or the loss of a loved one. In such times of prayer, our deeper motives may also surface. Sometimes, too, we feel God is silent in the midst of such crises. In this story, Abraham suddenly finds God telling him about a crisis that will soon overtake the city in which his nephew lives. There then follows a remarkable conversation.

1. In what ways do you think God might appear to behave or act unreasonably or unfairly?

2. Read Genesis 18:16-33. From the evidence in the passage, describe the relationship that exists between Abraham and God.

How does this affect the way God behaves toward Abraham?

3. How and what we pray usually reflects our motives for praying; from this passage, what do you think Abraham was most concerned about?

4. In verses 16-17, God appears to initiate the conversation with Abraham, and in verse 33 he ends it. How does this match up with your own experiences in prayer?

5. What motivates you to pray for other people, especially those who do not follow Christ?

6. A recurrent theme in the passage is the fact that God appears to be planning to simultaneously destroy the righteous and the wicked. Abraham refers to this several times (vv. 23-24, 28, 29, 30, 31 and 32). Why does he repeatedly bring up the issue?

7. From the passage what are the distinctive characteristics of an intercessor?

8. God does not appear to be angry with Abraham for asking questions—even when he appears to question God's justice. How does this give us reassurance when we pray in difficult or confusing circumstances?

9. God still went on to destroy Sodom and Gomorrah (you can read the rest of the story in chapter 19). What thoughts and feelings might Abraham have gone through after his conversation with God had ended?

10. This passage highlights a further aspect of prayer we easily forget—that God may speak to us in prayer. List and discuss ways in which you have experienced God guiding and prompting you in prayer, or changing your views as you pray.

11. Abraham listened to God and as a consequence learned more about him. How, practically, can we ensure that we try to listen to God when we pray?

12. For the next week, deliberately set aside a brief time each day to listen to God by meditating on a passage of Scripture. If you are meeting with a group, discuss what you have learned at the next meeting.

2
Discovering God's Will: Moses

Exodus 32:1-14

Sometimes we may wonder if prayer changes anything. "If God has his plans, and will work out his purposes, do we really need to pray?"

In this passage we see Moses the intercessor at work. Intercession is prayer on behalf of those deserving God's judgment. Abraham in the previous study interceded too; but Moses' prayer of intercession in this passage has a different (although equally significant) result.

1. When you pray about friends or families who are unbelievers, what do you usually pray for them?

2. Read Exodus 32:1-14. Why do you think Israel made a golden calf to worship?

3. How does God feel about the Israelites' worship of the golden calf (vv. 7-10, 12)? Why?

4. In what way(s) does the idea of God judging people for their sin affect the way you pray for people?

5. What does the passage show us about Moses' character and priorities as an intercessor?

6. Given the actions of the Israelites (vv. 1-6), if you were Moses, how would you have responded to God's offer in verse 10 to make him a great nation?

7. Verse 11 shows Moses' reaction to God's command to stand aside in verse 10. What internal conflicts or divided loyalties might Moses have felt as he spoke to God?

8. What personal risk(s) does Moses' prayer involve?

9. Moses appeals to God not to destroy the children of Israel (vv. 11-13), reminding God of his promises in Scripture. Why do you think he made his appeal to God in this way?

10. Why do you think God chose to follow an alternative course of action (v. 14) to that which he originally outlined (v. 10)?

11. Summarize what the passage teaches us about prayer and its importance.

12. Who do you need to ask God to have mercy for?

13. List people for whom and situations about which you can begin to intercede on a regular basis. Keep a record of the answers to prayer and any guidance about how to pray received from God. If you are meeting with a group, in two or three weeks discuss how your prayer for the person or situation is changing, and what has happened as result of praying.

3
Answered Prayer: Nehemiah

Nehemiah 1:1—2:8

If I ask a group of Christians what they find difficult about prayer, one of the issues usually raised is "Why aren't my prayers answered?" Sometimes it is our unwillingness to be obedient to God that means our prayers are not answered. And, sometimes, we are not prepared to let God use us to answer our prayers.

Jerusalem, the location of the temple of God, was to the Old Testament believer the center of their devotion (as it is for Jews today). Nehemiah, a Jew in exile, was a senior official in the Persian royal court, strategically placed to be part of the answer to his prayer for the rebuilding of Jerusalem.

1. How does what you feel about something or someone affect the way you pray?

2. Read Nehemiah 1:1—2:8. What motive(s) ultimately prompts Nehemiah to approach the king (1:2-3)?

3. In 1:4 Nehemiah reacts strongly to the news brought to him in 1:2-3. How might Nehemiah's feelings have affected the way he then prayed?

4. Look carefully at the lengths of time (1:1; 2:1) over which Nehemiah prayed. Why might Nehemiah have had to (or wanted to) pray for a long time about the issues that concerned him?

5. Nehemiah 1:5 shows us the first stage of Nehemiah's prayer. How can focusing on God at the beginning of our prayers enable us to pray with more confidence?

6. Nehemiah's prayer then goes on to repentance (1:6-7), not only for his own sin but also his people's wrongdoing. Why might he have felt the need to both repent personally and identify with the sin of others?

7. For what reasons might Nehemiah have returned to God's promises and previous dealings with the children of Israel (1:8-10) as part of his prayer?

8. Nehemiah 1:11 and 2:4 give us an understanding of how Nehemiah saw God in control over the circumstances he faced. How does our understanding of God's sovereignty affect the way we pray for situations?

9. In 1:11—2:8 we see Nehemiah taking steps to tackle the problem of Jerusalem's walls being broken down (1:3). In light of the enormous human and practical odds Nehemiah was up against, what do you think gave him confidence to embark on the task God had given him to do?

10. Nehemiah's fear in 2:2 indicates the risks he was taking in approaching the king on this issue. Why do you think Nehemiah was allowed to speak and ask for help?

11. What does Nehemiah's request show us about his thinking and prayer prior to his audience with the king?

12. What lessons from Nehemiah's prayers help you in your own prayer life?

13. During the next week, write down what you pray for each day and, next to that, note practical ways in which you could be involved in answering your own prayers. If you are studying with a group, discuss what you have learned from the exercise in the next meeting.

4
Prayer and Spiritual Conflict: Daniel

Daniel 10

Christians often react in one of two ways to spiritual conflict. They assume everything stems from it and become unhealthily fascinated by it. Or they don't think it's a problem. Seeing spiritual conflict in the way God sees it is critical. Daniel 10 not only teaches us more about intercession and intercessors, but also gives us a rare insight into the realities of the heavenly places, and a hint of the importance of our prayer in such situations.

1. Some Christians can identify times in their lives when they have felt very close to God. If you have had such an experience, what has been its lasting impact on your Christian discipleship?

2. Read Daniel 10. What can you tell about the character of Daniel from the passage?

3. Daniel received a message from God concerning a great war. He then

refused to eat certain foods and mourned for a period of three weeks (vv. 2-3).
Why do you think he did this?

From the fact of his partial fast, it appears that Daniel took the idea of fasting
seriously. What place should it have in our prayer lives?

4. The description of the "man" Daniel saw in verses 5-6 is very similar to John's
description of Christ in Revelation 1:13-15. Or it may have been an angel. Even
though Daniel had received a visit from a heavenly being before, this was still
a very unusual occurrence. Why do you think God went to this length to
communicate with Daniel?

5. Daniel was dramatically affected by the revelation he received (see vv. 8-9
and 15-17). What does the passage teach us about the way in which God deals
with us?

6. What lasting effects do you think Daniel's experience had on his relationship
with God?

7. We often interpret world events on a purely human level. God reveals to
Daniel that there is a spiritual battle going on behind the scenes for his people

(vv. 13, 20, 21). What evidence is there in the passage of the effect of Daniel's prayer on this spiritual battle in the heavenly places?

8. Note that Daniel does not directly fight with the satanic forces referred to ("the prince of the Persian kingdom" [v. 13], "the prince of Persia . . . the prince of Greece" [v. 20]). How does this reassure us when we think about spiritual warfare?

9. How does what the "man" (or angel) says in the passage help us to understand God's role in human history?

10. How does Daniel's prayer and consequent involvement in spiritual conflict help us to realize that our prayer makes a difference—even if we don't fully understand the implications?

11. How can we ensure that our understanding of what we pray for has as clear a spiritual or heavenly perspective as possible?

12. Decide on two or three world situations for which you want to pray by yourself or with a group. Remember to pray about these regularly.

5
Praying for the Nation: Ezekiel

Ezekiel 22:23-31

Have you ever wondered what Jesus would say about your nation if he walked through its streets today?

Ezekiel, a priest, was called by God to warn his people of God's judgment. Already humiliated in defeat by the Babylonians, Judah was spiritually bankrupt. Like most of his fellow citizens, Ezekiel lived in exile amidst idolatry and materialism. His people, his nation and its leaders paid lip service to their beliefs, but led lives that were far from pleasing to God. The passage is the third of three warnings in chapter 22 alone about the sin of Jerusalem and its people.

1. In what ways do you think that Christians' influence on national life could be greater than it is?

2. Read Ezekiel 22:23-31. Rain (v. 24) is probably a symbol of God's grace and kindness. Its absence suggests that Jerusalem and Judah are a spiritual "desert." God has almost withdrawn his presence from the land and is angry at the sins he sees. List the sins which have brought God to the point where he wishes to execute judgment.

3. Societies are interdependent. What we do affects others. How would the moral failure of each of the five groups mentioned in the passage (princes, prophets, priests, officials and people) affect the other four groups?

---

4. The priests would have been the principle intercessors. How would their shortcomings (v. 26) have affected their prayer for the nation?

---

5. The prophets (in Old Testament times those who spoke God's truth into specific situations) were failing to fulfill their responsibilities (v. 28). What do you think motivated them to behave as they did?

---

6. What moral qualities do you think the spiritual and secular leaders of a nation should possess?

---

7. The phrase "stand before me in the gap" (v. 30) is symbolic of intercession in the Old Testament. The absence of an intercessor had catastrophic consequences. Why do you think no one wanted to intercede?

How do you think intercession can affect world events today?

8. Not finding anyone to take positive action to set the nation back on course (to "build up the wall" as Nehemiah did) is seen by God as a problem as serious as having no intercessor. Alongside prayer, what else is necessary for Christians to be a godly influence on their nation?

9. Christians in some countries feel they can have no impact on the life of their nation because they are so few in number. How can this passage encourage believers in such a situation?

10. We often blame our national "leaders." Clearly from this passage all groups in society bear responsibility for the state of the nation. How should this affect the way we intercede for and live in our nations?

11. How is God calling you to stand in the gap?

12. Spend time praying for various national leaders. You might use information from newspapers or magazines to help you pray in a more informed way.

6
Praying for Everyone: Paul

1 Timothy 2:1-8

Wwhat was it like to be involved in the early church? Acts tells us what was central to its life: Bible teaching, practical fellowship, the sacraments and prayer. The early believers demonstrated social responsibility, were respected by outsiders and daily saw people come to Christ (Acts 2:42-47). Often our church life falls far short of the biblical ideal. Prayer needs its rightful place in the agenda.

In this passage we find the apostle Paul addressing various issues concerning the church and its worship. Interestingly, Paul addresses the issue of prayer first—as one of primary importance to the early church in Ephesus in which Timothy was involved. The issues Paul discusses also provide us with a framework in which to review what we have learned in the studies so far.

1. Why is prayer important? (Use what you have learned from studies 1-5 to respond.)

2. Read 1 Timothy 2:1-8. What reasons does Paul give in the passage for the importance of prayer?

3. Apart from giving instruction on prayer, Paul also discusses essential Christian doctrines in verses 4-6. What do you think Paul is implying here about the relationship between prayer and doctrine?

4. Paul encourages us to pray for all people, but then highlights a particular example (v. 2). Why is prayer for such people important? (You may also want to draw on studies 3-5 in your response.)

5. Paul seems to be saying that good leaders and bad leaders need the same approach—we have to pray for them all. Looking at studies 1-2, what attitudes do intercessors demonstrate toward the people they pray for?

6. How do you think that prayer might lead to us live "peaceful and quiet lives in all godliness and holiness" (v. 2)?

7. Paul underlines (vv. 3, 6) that God longs for all to come to know him through Christ—even though many will reject him. What have studies 1-6 taught you or reinforced for you about praying for non-Christians?

8. Why do you think prayer is "good, and pleases God our Savior" (v. 3)? (Draw on what you have been learning in these studies.)

9. Paul emphasizes in verse 8 the godly moral integrity ("holy hands") and unity of believers. Why is this important if we are to pray as Paul directs?

10. Drawing on what you have seen in each of the people we have studied so far, what aspects of character are important in an intercessor?

11. What character quality would you most like to develop?

What steps do you need to take to do that?

12. Ask God to "teach you how to pray," asking him to help you in the areas in which you need to grow. If you are meeting with a group, spend some time praying together about the prayer lives of the group members, particularly what you all have been learning about prayer and areas of prayer in which you each need encouragement.

7
Relying on God: David
Psalm 5

Feeling betrayed, persecuted or fearful are common human experiences. Christians are not immune to such experiences. Indeed, because of the opposition of the fallen world to Christ, we will inevitably face them. How do we pray in these circumstances? Instead of allowing our fear or anger to dominate our thinking, we need to focus on God. Psalm 5 is one example of a prayer written in the face of opposition.

1. What happens to your relationship with God (especially your prayer life) when you find yourself facing pressure, opposition or persecution?

2. Read Psalm 5. Instead of dealing with his enemies by becoming aggressive or planning revenge, David turns to God in prayer. Summarize the requests David makes of God.

3. David is clearly accustomed to beginning his day with prayer (v. 3). What are the benefits of this model?

4. David appears confident that God hears his prayer (v. 3). What does he say about the character of God that would give him such confidence?

5. List the characteristics of the wicked and the righteous from David's descriptions in the passage.

6. How might David's understanding of God's judgment upon his present or future enemies (vv. 4-6 and 10) have affected the way David dealt with his enemies?

7. While David clearly sees his enemies as the source of his problems, he sees their sins as the heart of their rebellion against God (v. 10). How can this perspective help us to pray for those who oppose us or persecute us because of our faith?

8. How might David's description of God's view of evil (vv. 4, 10) help us when we feel like blaming God for pain or persecution?

9. David clearly saw God as his source of refuge (v. 11), protection (v. 11), blessing (v. 12) and as a "shield" (v. 12). In what ways do you think David's awareness of God in these terms helped him to remain faithful during the attacks on him?

10. What aspects of David's prayer in this passage are a helpful model for you?

11. Think of any situations that represent a threat or pressure for you. Spend some time praying about those situations, trying to focus particularly on God's power and supremacy over the situation (while being realistic about the difficulties!).

8
Being Honest with God: Hannah
1 Samuel 1

As you grow in maturity, God's will, God's purposes, God's honor will increasingly concern you. But however mature you may become, you will never cease to have griefs and joys of your own. If prayer that concerns God's honor is to be called higher prayer, I must make it clear that you must never stop appealing to God about your sorrows and heartaches. Lower prayer, if we adopt such an expression, will be necessary as long as you live. 'Have no anxiety about anything,' writes Paul to the Philippian church, 'but in everything by prayer and supplication with thanksgiving let your requests be made known to God' (Philippians 4:6)."[1]

1. In what ways has your experience of suffering strengthened your faith as a Christian?

2. Read 1 Samuel 1. What evidence is there in the passage of faithful and godly living by Elkanah and his family?

3. Many of the prayers studied so far are for other people—the lost, leaders and nations. List the ways in which this story illustrates the concern of God for individual believers and their needs.

4. We often feel conflict between what we want and what we think God wants, and we may have mixed motives when we pray as to why we pray for things. What internal conflicts or mixed motives might Hannah have experienced as she prayed?

How do you think the way that God answers prayer is affected by the purity of our motives?

5. Verse 5 is evidence that Hannah's prayer was initiated by God. When has God put you in a situation through which you now realize you were being prompted to pray?

6. Verses 10-16 demonstrate Hannah's honesty in prayer to God. She does not hide her feelings, pain, hurt or desire. What might prevent us from being this direct with God if we were in a similar situation?

7. It is often hard for us to understand other people's suffering. Eli's blessing in verse 17 is very different in tone from his initial reaction to Hannah in verses 13-14. How and why do his views of her change throughout the story?

8. According to the passage, how did Hannah view the child she was asking for?

_____

9. Samuel was one of the most significant leaders in Israel's history, and was born at a turning point in the history of the nation. How does God's use of Hannah's personal circumstances to bring about his wider objectives help us to understand the purpose of suffering?

_____

10. Compare verse 18 with verses 6-16. How do you explain Hannah's change of mood and apparent sense of assurance?

_____

11. Verses 21-28 detail the events after Hannah's prayer was answered. However, the actions of Hannah and Elkanah relate back to the promise Hannah made in verse 11. What does this teach us about their character as believers?

_____

12. When are you hesitant to take personal requests before God?

_____

13. Silently read and reflect on 1 Samuel 2:1-10. How are you encouraged by this passage? Spend some time thanking God for the things you have learned.

_____

[1] John White, _Daring_, pp. 85-86.

9
Thanking God: Mary
Luke 1:46-55

O ur rights—under the constitution—are very important to us. We (often justifiably) defend them jealously and assert them freely just as we guard our freedoms and privileges. We may, however, rarely stop to say thank you for any of them. We can even carry the same attitudes over into our Christian lives. Rights and freedoms can become more important than service and responsibility, success more valuable than obedience, status more spiritual than humility. We expect God's blessings because we deserve them.

Jesus' mother, Mary, had few rights and minimal privileges in her culture— and in her religion. And she was probably the last person to expect to be the mother of Christ. She does not applaud God for choosing her, or demand a reward for taking the job on. Instead, she prays, conscious of her God-given significance and the privilege of her calling.

1. In what sorts of circumstances do you find it difficult to thank God?

2. Read Luke 1:46-55. What does the passage show us about what Mary thought God was like?

3. What does the passage show us about how Mary saw herself before God?

4. Verses 46-47 tell us that Mary glorified the Lord and rejoiced in her Savior. In what ways can we do this in our prayers?

5. Verse 50 tells us that God's mercy extends to those who fear him. How does your "fear" of God affect the way that you pray to him?

6. Mary prayed in thankfulness for being chosen as Christ's mother. However, she also refers to many other actions of God in her prayer. What does this show us about her understanding of God?

7. Imagine you have a Christian friend who feels that God is remote from his or her situation and has no sense of God's presence in his or her daily life. Consequently, prayer is difficult. How can you help that person to pray?

8. In what ways do verses 51-53 both reassure us and act as a warning to us?

9. In verses 54-55, Mary speaks of God acting consistently with what he had previously promised. How can the ways that God has fulfilled his biblical promises be a basis for thanksgiving in our prayer lives?

10. How should praising and thanking God take a different place in your prayer life? Explain your answer.

11. Make a list of things that God has done in past history, and things that have happened in the last week, that you want to thank God for. (If you are meeting with a group, make a list together.) Spend some time in thanksgiving.

10
Blessing Other People: Paul

Ephesians 1:15-23 and 3:14-21

Dear Hillary," Beth began, "Thanks so much for your letter. I'm really sorry to hear that the way ahead seems so confusing and that you find the lack of obvious guidance so hard to deal with. I want to reassure you that I do pray for you and that I ask God to clearly guide you as to the next step in your career. I pray that the Lord will bless you."

Beth put her pen down. "Bless?" she thought. "What do I mean? Hillary is in such a difficult situation that I don't know what is best to pray for her. If I just say 'bless,' it sounds like I can't be bothered to think of anything else. What will she think? What does God want me to pray? If I say 'bless,' will he know what I mean?"

It's not easy to know how to pray for a friend in need. In this passage we see how Paul prays for his friends.

1. How do you decide what to pray for another person?

2. Read Ephesians 1:15-23 and 3:14-21. What seems to be Paul's motive in praying for those he is writing to?

3. What themes run through Paul's prayers in the two passages?

4. Ephesians 1:15-23 refers back to 1:3-14 (thus the expression "for this reason" in verse 15). Look briefly at that section of Scripture. What does this tell you about the source of Paul's prayer requests?

5. Like any group of Christians, the churches Paul wrote to must have contained difficult or rebellious Christians—maybe even Christians who did not like Paul. Despite this, Paul gives thanks for them all in 1:16. Why could Paul still do this and pray for them as he did?

6. Look specifically at what Paul prays in 1:17-19. Describe effects on the lives of the believers that you think Paul's prayers might have brought about.

If Paul has been praying for non-Christians, in what ways would his requests have been different?

7. In the latter part of 1:19 Paul concentrates on God's demonstration of his power through the death and resurrection of Christ. Why do you think he does this?

8. Turn to 3:14-21. How do Paul's words emphasize or illustrate the depth of relationship with God that he wanted to see in the Ephesian believers?

Why might he so strongly stress this depth of relationship (or intimacy) with God?

9. Paul considers the love of Christ (3:16-19). Why is it important for you to be conscious of Christ's love in your daily life?

10. Ephesians 3:20 reminds us of God's power and supremacy. How should our understanding of God's ability to change people and circumstances affect the way we pray?

11. Paul clearly longed for these Christians to grow in their relationship with God—and prayed accordingly. How, specifically, can Paul's example help us to pray for those around us?

12. Using the central themes of Paul's prayer as a basis, spend time praying for other Christians that you know, or, if you are meeting with a group, you can pray for each other.

11
Praying Together: The Early Church

Acts 4:23-31

One of the marks of the early church was that they prayed together—to great effect. The missionary activity of the early believers continued to grow as they prayed together (Acts 2:42) and as the Lord empowered them to evangelize.

But what were their prayer meetings like? Acts 4 gives us the opportunity to listen in on one of the early church's prayer meetings, to see how and what they prayed for. The New Testament letters and the practice of the early church underline the place of group prayer and its importance. Likewise, it should be one activity we emphasize in the church today.

1. Some people enjoy praying with other Christians, while others find it a terrifying experience. What contribution to your Christian life and witness has praying with other Christians made?

2. Read Acts 4:23-31. Peter and John have just been released from imprisonment by the religious authorities for preaching about Christ and performing a miracle. In what way(s) is the early church's response to such persecution surprising?

3. What does the passage teach us about the unity of the believers?

---

4. In what ways can praying with other Christians build unity?

---

5. List the aspects of God's character that appear to be in the minds of the believers as they pray.

How would concentrating on the character of God help the believers get a perspective on the persecution they faced?

---

6. Sometimes we find events in the world confusing; for example, when evil seems to triumph over good. What can we learn from verses 24-28 to help us understand such situations?

---

7. Look at the requests in verses 29-30. What do they teach us about the believers' priorities and attitudes?

8. Not all answers to prayers are dramatic, but the believers' prayer was clearly answered (v. 31). Sometimes we can be surprised by how God answers our prayers. Why do you think this is?

9. Verse 31 tells us that a deeper experience of the Holy Spirit enabled the church to be bold in its evangelism. How does this compare with what Christians often desire from their experience of the Holy Spirit?

10. What do you find difficult about praying with others? (If you are meeting with a group, talk specifically about your group.)

What would help you with group prayer?

11. Pray about specific situations in evangelism that you face, especially where boldness is required.

12
Praying with Confidence: Jesus
Luke 11:1-13

Confidence is a vital factor in human relationships. The confidence that we can trust our friends—to keep a promise or to help us out in difficult circumstances—enables us to feel secure. And, more importantly, it enables our friendships to grow in an environment of openness.

Trust should characterize our relationship with God. Even though we let him down, he wants us to live in the knowledge that he is absolutely reliable. He hears our prayers, longs to answer them in accordance with his will, and is totally fair.

1. What aspects of prayer would you most like reassurance about?

2. Read Luke 11:1-13. What different aspects of prayer do you see included in the prayer in verses 2-4?

In what ways do the different aspects and emphases in the prayer provide a model for your own prayer life?

3. Why do you think the friend overcomes his initial reluctance to help his neighbor (vv. 5-8)?

4. The friend gives his neighbor "as much as he needs" in answer to his request (v. 8). What does this passage teach us about the answers we receive to our prayers?

5. Luke 11:9-10 considers the issue of persistence in prayer. How does the passage help us to understand what "persistence in prayer" involves?

6. Jesus teaches on prayer because a disciple asks for teaching in verse 1. In Luke 18:1 he reminds them that "they should always pray and not give up." We are all tempted not to pray—or stop praying when we should pray. In what practical ways can we resist such temptation?

7. In what ways does this passage help you to be more confident about prayer?

8. Studies 1-6 concentrated on examples of intercession. What other types of prayer have you learned about in studies 7-12?

9. To what extent does your prayer life reflect a healthy balance between the different types of prayer?

10. How has your understanding of praying when faced with opposition or persecution changed as a result of studies 7 and 11?

11. What practical steps do you need to take (individually or as a group) to develop your prayer life?

12. Pray about the aspects of prayer for which you feel the need for reassurance, following up on any issues raised by questions 1 and 11.

Leader's Notes

Leading a Bible discussion can be an enjoyable and rewarding experience. But it can also be *scary*—especially if you've never done it before. If this is your feeling, you're in good company. When God asked Moses to lead the Israelites out of Egypt, he replied, "O Lord, please send someone else to do it!" (Ex 4:13).

When Solomon became king of Israel, he felt the task was beyond his abilities. "I am only a little child and do not know how to carry out my duties. . . . Who is able to govern this great people of yours?" (1 Kings 3:7, 9).

When God called Jeremiah to be a prophet, he replied, "Ah, Sovereign LORD, . . . I do not know how to speak; I am only a child" (Jer 1:6).

The list goes on. The apostles were "unschooled, ordinary men" (Acts 4:13). Timothy was young, frail and frightened. Paul's "thorn in the flesh" made him feel weak. But God's response to all of his servants—including you—is essentially the same: "My grace is sufficient for you" (2 Cor 12:9). Relax. God helped these people in spite of their weaknesses, and he can help you in spite of your feelings of inadequacy.

There is another reason why you should feel encouraged. Leading a Bible discussion is not difficult if you follow certain guidelines. You don't need to be an expert on the Bible or a trained teacher. The suggestions listed below should enable you to effectively and enjoyably fulfill your role as leader.

Preparing to Lead

1. Ask God to help you understand and apply the passage to your own life. Unless this happens, you will not be prepared to lead others. Pray too for the various members of the group. Ask God to give you an enjoyable and profitable time together studying his Word.

2. As you begin each study, read and reread the assigned Bible passage to familiarize yourself with what the author is saying. In the case of book studies, you may want to read through the entire book prior to the first study. This will give you a helpful overview of its contents.

3. This study guide is based on the New International Version of the Bible. It will help you and the group if you use this translation as the basis for your study and discussion. Encourage others to use the NIV also, but allow them the freedom to use whatever translation they prefer.

4. Carefully work through each question in the study. Spend time in meditation and reflection as you formulate your answers.

5. Write your answers in the space provided in the study guide. This will help you to express your understanding of the passage clearly.

6. It might help you to have a Bible dictionary handy. Use it to look up any unfamiliar words, names or places. (For additional help on how to study a passage, see chapter five of *Leading Bible Discussions,* IVP.)

7. Once you have finished your own study of the passage, familiarize yourself with the leader's notes for the study you are leading. These are designed to help you in several ways. First, they tell you the purpose the study guide author had in mind while writing the study. Take time to think through how the study questions work together to accomplish that purpose. Second, the notes provide you with additional background information or comments on some of the questions. This information can be useful if people have difficulty understanding or answering a question. Third, the leader's notes can alert you to potential problems you may encounter during the study.

8. If you wish to remind yourself of anything mentioned in the leader's notes, make a note to yourself below that question in the study.

Leading the Study

1. Begin the study on time. Unless you are leading an evangelistic Bible study, open with prayer, asking God to help you to understand and apply the passage.

2. Be sure that everyone in your group has a study guide. Encourage them to prepare beforehand for each discussion by working through the questions in the guide.

3. At the beginning of your first time together, explain that these studies are meant to be discussions not lectures. Encourage the members of the group to participate. However, do not put pressure on those who may be hesitant to speak during the first few sessions.

4. Read the introductory paragraph at the beginning of the discussion. This will orient the group to the passage being studied.

5. Read the passage aloud if you are studying one chapter or less. You may choose to do this yourself, or someone else may read if he or she has been asked to do so prior to the study. Longer passages may occasionally be read in parts at different times during the study. Some studies may cover several chapters. In such cases reading aloud would probably take too much time, so the group members should simply read the assigned passages prior to the study.

6. As you begin to ask the questions in the guide, keep several things in mind. First, the questions are designed to be used just as they are written. If you wish, you may simply read them aloud to the group. Or you may prefer to express them in your own words. However, unnecessary rewording of the questions is not recommended.

Second, the questions are intended to guide the group toward understanding and applying the *main idea* of the passage. The author of the guide has stated his or her view of this central idea in the *purpose* of the study in the leader's notes. You should try to understand how the passage expresses this idea and how the study questions work together to lead the group in that direction.

There may be times when it is appropriate to deviate from the study guide. For example, a question may have already been answered. If so, move on to the next question. Or someone may raise an important question not covered in the guide. Take time to discuss it! The important thing is to use discretion. There may be many routes you can travel to reach the goal of the study. But the easiest route is usually the one the author has suggested.

7. Avoid answering your own questions. If necessary, repeat or rephrase them until they are clearly understood. An eager group quickly becomes passive and silent if they think the leader will do most of the talking.

8. Don't be afraid of silence. People may need time to think about the question before formulating their answers.

9. Don't be content with just one answer. Ask, "What do the rest of you think?" or "Anything else?" until several people have given answers to the question.

10. Acknowledge all contributions. Try to be affirming whenever possible. Never reject an answer. If it is clearly wrong, ask, "Which verse led you to that conclusion?" or again, "What do the rest of you think?"

11. Don't expect every answer to be addressed to you, even though this will probably happen at first. As group members become more at ease, they will begin to truly interact with each other. This is one sign of a healthy discussion.

12. Don't be afraid of controversy. It can be very stimulating. If you don't resolve an issue completely, don't be frustrated. Move on and keep it in mind for later. A subsequent study may solve the problem.

13. Stick to the passage under consideration. It should be the source for answering the questions. Discourage the group from unnecessary cross-referencing. Likewise, stick to the subject and avoid going off on tangents.

14. Periodically summarize what the *group* has said about the passage. This helps to draw together the various ideas mentioned and gives continuity to the study. But don't preach.

15. Conclude your time together with conversational prayer. Be sure to ask God's help to apply those things which you learned in the study.

16. End on time.

Many more suggestions and helps are found in *Leading Bible Discussions* (IVP). Reading and studying through that would be well worth your time.

Components of Small Groups

A healthy small group should do more than study the Bible. There are four components you should consider as you structure your time together.

Nurture. Being a part of a small group should be a nurturing and edifying experience. You should grow in your knowledge and love of God and each other. If we are to properly love God, we must know and keep his commandments (Jn 14:15). That is why Bible study should be a foundational part of your small group. But you can be nurtured by other things as well. You can memorize Scripture, read and discuss a book, or occasionally listen to a tape of a good speaker.

Community. Most people have a need for close friendships. Your small group can be an excellent place to cultivate such relationships. Allow time for informal interaction before and after the study. Have a time of sharing during the meeting. Do fun things together as a group, such as a potluck supper or a picnic. Have someone bring refreshments to the meeting. Be creative!

Worship. A portion of your time together can be spent in worship and prayer. Praise God together for who he is. Thank him for what he has done and is doing in your lives and in the world. Pray for each other's needs. Ask God to help you to apply what you have learned. Sing hymns together.

Mission. Many small groups decide to work together in some form of outreach. This can be a practical way of applying what you have learned. You can host a series of evangelistic discussions for your friends or neighbors. You can visit people at a home for the elderly. Help a widow with cleaning or repair jobs around her home. Such projects can have a transforming influence on your group.

For a detailed discussion of the nature and function of small groups, read *Small Group Leaders' Handbook* or *Good Things Come in Small Groups* (both from IVP).

Study 1. Conversing with God. Genesis 18:16-33.

Purpose: To see that prayer is initiated by God. We pray because God wants us to, not because we have to do it to gain his favor.

General Note. This passage underlines the two-way nature of prayer, and introduces the idea of intercession (praying on behalf of those deserving God's judgment). Prayer can change our understanding of God, which may in some circumstances be more important than getting the "answer" we seek to our prayer.

Background. Around 2000 B.C. Abraham and Sarah are visited by three strangers (the Lord himself and two angels). Abraham and Sarah are promised a child (remarkable given their ages—see Gen 18:11). Then the visitors are about to depart, where the story takes up in verse 16.

Question 1. Every study begins with an "approach" question, which is meant to be asked before the passage is read. These questions are important for several reasons.

First, they help the group to warm up to each other. No matter how well a group may know each other, there is always a stiffness that needs to be overcome before people will begin to talk openly. A good question will break the ice.

Second, approach questions get people thinking along the lines of the topic of the study. Most people will have lots of different things going on in their minds (dinner, an important meeting coming up, how to get the car fixed) that will have nothing to do with the study. A creative question will get their attention and draw them into the discussion.

Third, approach questions can reveal where our thoughts or feelings need to be transformed by Scripture. That is why it is especially important not to read the passage before the approach question is asked. The passage will tend to color the honest reactions people would otherwise give because they are, of course, supposed to think the way the Bible does. Giving honest responses before they find out what the Bible says may help them see where their thoughts or attitudes need to be changed.

This question helps us think about the way we react to God's actions when we do not understand what he is doing. As you explore the passage, you will see Abraham grappling with God's justice and the idea of judgment. Remember as you discuss that as God is perfect and without sin, his actions are similarly perfect, however much we might feel like blaming him! Encourage the group to discuss how their view of God (for example, if they think he is unfair) affects the way they pray to him.

Question 2. Abraham and God "knew" each other well. This may contrast strongly with our relationship with God. Abraham is treated as a friend, with whom God is prepared to share his plans and purposes. Encourage the group to realize that we are in a similar privileged position—God wants us actively involved in his purposes.

Question 3. Look at verses 23 and 25. Note that despite Lot and his family living in the city (one concern) Abraham did not allow his personal involvement to eclipse his longing to see God's justice being done and being seen to be done (his other concern).

Question 4. The focus of Abraham's prayer shifts from discussing his future child (first part of chapter 18) to God's justice and mercy. God shifts the agenda of Abraham's prayer; God also, it appears, prompts him to pray and ends the prayer time. We often approach prayer as if it is our "job"—however, it is both divine initiative and human response. Discuss the group members' experiences of how God has prompted them to pray, or to stop praying, about a specific issue (God won't, of course, tell us not to pray at all!). Sometimes, also, we talk so much in prayer we do not give God a chance to speak. Abraham did not do this. The conversation was genuinely two-way.

Abraham, of course, may have thought he initiated the conversation with God, whereas looking back it is clear that God did initiate the prayer. So it may appear to us in our prayer lives.

Question 5. The need to understand why we intercede is essential in evangelism. In intercession we are involved in God's plan for those around us. If we see it as important, we will pray more.

Question 6. John White, in *Daring to Draw Near,* comments: "His prayer is not, as some scholars suggest, a mere reflection of the bargaining practices among traders in the East. Abraham has nothing to offer in trade with God. Moreover the stakes are too high. He is not haggling with God. He is desperate to understand" (p. 19).

Abraham is (reverently and fearfully) probing God's character and justice. He wants to know what God is like and why he is doing this. As a general point on the passage, some in the group may find it difficult to accept the idea that God is not neutral about those who reject him; those who reject God's offer of salvation in Christ are under his judgment and are separated from him.

Question 7. Abraham, to risk questioning God, must have been prepared to be selfless. Common characteristics of prayers of intercession are concern for God's glory and reputation (for example, "Will not the Judge of all the earth do right?" v. 25) and concern for people under God's judgment ("Will you sweep away the righteous with the wicked?" v. 23).

Question 8. That God is willing to be on the receiving end of probing questions should give us reassurance in prayer. We are free to express our feelings, even our doubts; God can take it!

Question 9. It is often disillusioning for us not to have our prayer answered in the way we expect. John White comments as follows:

> Why did Abraham stop at ten? We may never know. One thing is certain. He was reassured. As each response came back at him, "For the sake of forty I will not do it. . . . I will not do it, if I find thirty there. . . . For the sake of ten I will not destroy it . . ." the image of God was changing in Abraham's eyes. It was no monster that faced him, but the familiar God of the covenant. Yet somehow God was larger. He was less comprehensible. And, paradoxically, he was a God Abraham understood better than ever before. A familiar God whom yet he scarcely knew. A righteous God whose judgments were past finding out. (*Daring*, p. 21)

Questions 10-11. Direct verbal communication with God is exceptional! Remember that this is an unusual prayer in the sense that Abraham is literally face to face with God, and appears to get immediate responses to his questions. Do not let the unusual circumstances cover up the important general principles about prayer, especially its two-way nature. As the group discusses how God speaks and prompts, bear in mind that God's leading will never be inconsistent with his revealed truth in Scripture, and must always be weighed against it. While God spoke in a direct audible way to many biblical figures, because we have the Bible (which they did not, in its complete form) we have constant access to God's words. Accordingly, his normal way of conveying his truth to us is through the Bible; the Bible is described technically as "sufficient"; that is, it gives us enough teaching to be able to know God and obey him. Of course, being indwelt by a living God means that we will feel the presence of God, and he will certainly prompt and guide us experientially but always in ways consistent with the Bible. (There is no encouragement in the New Testament to search for new truth beyond that set down in the Old Testament and in the apostolic teaching which forms what we now call the New Testament. See also Jude 3.) The day to day process by which we make decisions is, generally, by using our minds, under the direction of the Spirit renewing our minds and consciences (Rom 12:2; see also pp. 12-13 of *Daring to Draw Near*). Growing in prayer and praying more biblically involves having our minds renewed so we think more in line with what God wants.

Question 12. Christian meditation involves filling our minds with God, for example, through reflecting on a passage of the Bible, in contrast to the Eastern mystic/New Age meditation of emptying our minds. It would be wise to agree on one or two passages from the Bible so the group has a focus for its learning. You could use one of the next study passages.

Background reading: John White, *Daring,* chapter 1. Joyce Baldwin, *The Message of Genesis 12-50* (Downers Grove, Ill.: InterVarsity Press, 1986)

Study 2. Discovering God's Will. Exodus 32:1-14.

Purpose: To further explore the nature of intercession, the character of an intercessor and the role of intercession in God's purposes.

Background. Moses, leader of the Israelites, is on Mount Sinai, and the children of Israel are below, under the leadership of Aaron. It is only recently that the Israelites had enthusiastically accepted the terms of God's covenant and promised obedience to his laws.

Question 1. Depending on the members of the group, you may find that people do not pray for those around them who are unbelievers. (You may also need to discuss this sensitively—or even omit the question—if your group contains unbelievers.) Try to discover how specific people are in what they pray. Your discussion may highlight issues that need to be discussed outside the confines of this study. An alternative approach question is "When you pray for friends or families who are clearly being disobedient to God, what do you pray for them?"

Question 2. We like to worship things and people that we can see and feel—it seems easier than worshiping a supernatural and invisible God. Despite their acceptance of God's laws and a pledge of obedience to them, within weeks the Israelites are breaking their promises to God. They make a replica of the gods they saw in Egypt, desiring the same sort of god to worship as their pagan neighbors. Having a calf (probably a more accurate translation is a "young bull") (Alan Cole, *Exodus,* Tyndale Old Testament Commentary [Downers Grove, Ill.: InterVarsity Press, 1973], p. 214) to worship may have reminded them of the sacred bull of Egypt, Apis, or a representation of the Canaanite god Baal.

Question 3. Contrast the first commandment in Exodus 20:3.

Question 4. This may create a discussion as to whether or not people feel that God's judgment is unfair or unnecessary. Try to stick to the question. Bear in mind that God would be unjust if he left sin unpunished. Sometimes we think other people deserve God's judgment more than we do and are tempted to look down on them (especially those who do not know Christ), feeling morally and/or spiritually superior to them. This affects both the way we pray for them and our prayers, because we are proud.

Question 5. These qualities are typical of the pattern of Old Testament intercessors: reverent fear, boldness, concern for people, concern for God's glory and reputation, and a preparedness to make sacrifices—even at great personal risk.

Question 6. It is possible that by making such an offer to Moses, God is in fact testing Moses' integrity to see if he puts God's purposes first or his own selfish desires.

Question 7. Encourage the group to imagine themselves in Moses' position and to think of his desires and loyalties. What might Moses be thinking about? How to rid himself of the troublesome Israelites, his own position as a leader, God's image and reputation on the eyes of the surrounding peoples, and God's reaction to Moses' questioning of God are likely to have been prominent in his thinking. The group may find it helpful to imagine how Moses felt. He would have had to be ruthlessy honest about his own ambitions before he could pray honestly to God.

Question 8. Moses appears to risk even disobeying God's command in verse 10 (presumably at the risk of his life) in the interests of his people. This is a curious situation, because serving God always comes over and above serving other people! The situation appears again to reflect the fact that Moses is being tested, just as God tested Abraham to see if he would sacrifice his son for God in Genesis 22.

Question 9. Moses could be certain of God's promises on the basis of the limited biblical material he had. His prayer was not based on subjective impressions of what he thought God might want to do, but on what God had definitely said. Moses can therefore ask with confidence. The promises and events Moses refers to in verses 12-13 are based on Genesis 12:7; 13:15; 15:5, 18; 17:8; 22:16-18; 26:4; 35:12; Exodus 13:5, 11; 33:1; Numbers 14:13-19; Deuteronomy 9:28 and Joshua 7:9. Indirectly, this passage underlines the value of Scripture as a basis for prayer.

Question 10. Try not to get sidetracked into complex discussions on sovereignty and free will in this question. As God is perfect he does not "change his mind" because he realizes he has made a mistake—nor just because he feels like it. God's behavior here is explained in human terms so that we can understand it. God embarked on a "different" course of action (for example, showing mercy) from that already proposed (judgment) due to a new factor—the prayer of Moses. Often in the Bible God's warnings and promises are conditional on men's and women's responses (for example, see Jn 1:12).

John in Revelation pictures prayers being brought into the presence of God in golden bowls, signifying their great importance to God. Clearly our prayers cannot be the place where we order God around, otherwise he would no longer be God. Here Moses has his views and desires bought into line with what God wants. (In a parallel way in the previous study Abraham discovered more about God.) Moses did not alter God's purpose for the children of Israel, but instead carried it out. He began to share God's mind and purpose more, as did Abraham.

Question 11. Discuss, if possible, how the lessons about intercession you learn in the group can be applied practically. How important we see prayer to be in carrying out God's purposes will change the way we pray. Equally, seeing prayer as a place where we learn about God and discover more of his purposes elevates its importance. If the group does not know each other well and is very reluctant to pray together, you could instead look at how the lessons from this study complement those learned in study one.

Question 12. One possibility is to encourage the group to pray on a regular basis for two or three non-Christian friends.

Background reading: John White, *Daring,* chapter 3. Alan Cole, *Exodus.*

Study 3. Answered Prayer. Nehemiah 1:1—2:8.

Purpose: Nehemiah's prayer teaches us about intercession that involves personal sacrifice and risk, shows how one man's concern can become that of many (a mark of prayer in God's will), and, as in Moses' prayer, is a model of identification with the sin of those you pray for.

Background. The story of Nehemiah is a continuation of the story told in Ezra, and begins around 446 B.C. Israel is in exile. Jerusalem was destroyed in 587 B.C. and most Jews were taken off into captivity to Babylon, in the Persian empire. The Jews had been permitted to return to Jerusalem, first between 538 and 516, and then under Ezra's leadership. Their attempts to rebuild the walls of Jerusalem were thwarted; the story is told in Ezra 4:7-23. The rebuilding is ultimately carried out by Nehemiah, permitted by the Persians' attitude of religious tolerance for those they had captured.

One issue highlighted in this study is that we must be prepared to be used by God to answer our own prayers. The group may need to be reminded that some prayers are not answered for reasons entirely outside of our control or influence. For instance, we may pray for friends to become Christians, but ultimately they have free will and choose whether or not to receive Christ—within the context of divine sovereignty.

Question 1. This question may bring out very different views of the place of emotion and feelings, which often reflect the personalities of the individuals. Bear in mind that prayer is a command. It is to be done whether or not we feel like it (although that may sometimes be very difficult). But feeling concern can help us to pray with enthusiasm—and may well reflect something of what God feels, if those feelings are in line with God's will. If our prayer life is dry, we need to pray for enthusiasm. If it is dependent only on "feelings," we need to pray for self-discipline. An additional question to stimulate further discussion would be "In what ways are we less effective in serving God if we don't feel what he feels about people or situations (or if we lack a vision of what he wants to do)?"

Question 2. "Like all his people, Nehemiah looked to Jerusalem as his heart's true home and the center round which his life revolved" (John White, *Excellence in Leadership* [Downers Grove, Ill.: InterVarsity Press, 1986], p. 14).

Nehemiah's concern to see Jerusalem rebuilt and restored was not based on nationalism or political ambition, but upon a desire to see true worship of his God at its heart, the temple, and out of shame that Jerusalem had been humiliated in judgment because of the Israelites' idolatry, materialism and unbelief.

Question 4. Note that the recorded words of Nehemiah would have only taken a minute or two to pray. We assume they represent a summary of a process of prayer. The month of Kislev (1:1) corresponds to mid-November through mid-December of 446 B.C. By the time Nehemiah has audience with the king (2:1), it is the month of Nisan (March-April 445 B.C.). We can only guess what Nehemiah may have gone through over this four-month period, and why God wished him to pray for this long period. God may have needed to bring Nehemiah to the point where he was prepared—or felt able—to be involved; or to enable him to reflect for a long time on what was the best course of action so that he did not rush into a course of action which would fail.

Question 6. Identification may seem a difficult concept for Westerners to understand. Our culture places high emphasis on individual responsibility. Nehemiah presumably saw himself as responsible as the next person for his nation's troubles.

Question 7. Note that again the intercessor returns to God's certain promises as a basis for prayer. Try to explore, if time permits, how much the group members use the Bible as part of their prayer lives.

Question 8. Note that Nehemiah does not only pray for God's help prior to the encounter with the king (1:11): he prays again in 2:4 when he is talking to him. This indicates his awareness of God's presence with him and reliance on him. Nehemiah's role as "cupbearer" meant he had access to the king that few others had. His role was to test the king's wine to ensure that it was not poisoned—a common cause of death of leaders in ancient times. Being sad in the king's presence was viewed as disapproval of the king himself, and usually resulted in death. Nehemiah is in a high-risk situation. This might have been his only chance to ask for permission.

Question 9. Nehemiah would have drawn strength from the promises and character of God (1:5-10), the prayers of others (1:11), and possibly the human circumstances he found himself in (1:11). There may have been other factors, such as confidence that God had heard his prayer, but we cannot identify this from the text.

Question 10. Nehemiah's trustworthiness (see notes to question 8) might have been a factor in the king's willingness to listen to him.

Question 11. Nehemiah used his mind to the fullest in the planning—note, for example, the detail in which Nehemiah had thought out his vision, requesting letters for safe-conduct and timber. Normally we think of "vision" as a very general, even vague, thing. Nehemiah, however, had both a clear vision of what God wanted him to do and a detailed strategy to achieve the task God had set out for him. Nehemiah's prayer changed too. Note particularly a move from a general concern to prayer for specific action. Initially, Nehemiah prayed alone, but by 1:11 others prayed also.

Question 12. Try to get the group to be as practical as possible in their application of the lessons from the passage. Spend some time praying together about what you have learned. One point the group might easily miss is that Nehemiah prayed an enormous amount before setting out on the task God had asked him to do. Often we only pray briefly or once we are in the midst of the situation and it is not working out the way we planned!

Question 13. This is optional, but may be helpful in getting group members to realize that they may pray for something (for example, that a friend may become a Christian) without being willing to be used by God to bring about the answer to their prayer (for example, by helping their friend to study the Bible).

Background reading: John White, *Excellence,* chapters 1-3. Derek Kidner, *Ezra and Nehemiah,* Tyndale Old Testament Commentary (Downers Grove, Ill.: InterVarsity Press, 1979).

Study 4. Prayer and Spiritual Conflict. Daniel 10.

Purpose: To examine the relationship between prayer and spiritual warfare. (The vision is principally discussed in chapter 11, so is not covered by this study.)

Background. The two southern Israelite tribes, called Judah, were conquered by the Babylonians in 586 B.C. Around 605 B.C. Daniel was taken along with other young Jews to work for the Babylonian authorities. From 605—536 B.C. the Jews were oppressed by the Babylonians and exiled, Jerusalem being destroyed. Then the Babylonians were overthrown by the Persians. Daniel lived through the exile of 70 years, and the story in chapter 10 occurs around the end of the exile (537 B.C.), when Daniel desires to know what will happen after the 70 years is over. Daniel 10-12 represents an insight into future world events, but is rather complex to interpret. (Try not to get involved in discussing complex theologies of the end times.) In brief, the vision predicts the messianic age (10:14), the future events involving Babylon and Greece (11:2-20), Antiochus, and the antichrist (11:21—12:3).

One question which might arise in group discussion is the meaning and purpose of a "vision," especially if some in the group are unfamiliar with them, or if they come from a church background which has strong views on what role visions have today.

Daniel's vision was given to explain a "revelation" (see 10:1). A revelation is when something is revealed—in this case a message from God. Daniel has a vision, either of God or an angelic being. Both in Old Testament times and now such encounters are exceptional, as were Abraham's and Moses' "face to face" encounters with God. It is helpful to set such events in the context of how God speaks to us in general. Early believers such as Daniel did not have the Bible in its completed form as we do. Part of the way the Bible came to us was through such events as Daniel's vision and the instruction that came through the vision. God used such events to reveal himself to us; what Daniel experienced has been recorded for us as authoritative biblical teaching.

As we have the completed Bible (the "canon"), the role of a vision today, were a believer to have one, is bound to be different. This does not mean that visions today are of no value; rather that they have a different purpose—for example, to edify or warn the believer, rather than to contribute to the canon of Scripture as Daniel's vision did. Their purpose is less significant, just as New Testament prophecy is not of the same status as the Old Testament prophecy of, say, Jeremiah. As with prophecy, dreams and our thinking, visions today must be weighed against Scripture as the final authority in all matters of faith and conduct. Visions are of course by nature subjective and transient. How you interpret a vision depends on who interprets it; you cannot go back and look again at the vision to see what it depicted. Scripture, in contrast, has objectivity and permanence. For a more comprehensive discussion, see Roy Clements's chapters on "Word and Spirit" in *Hear the Word,* ed. John White

(Leicester, U.K.: Inter-Varsity Press, 1990). Also it is a characteristic of spiritual experiences like the vision in Daniel 10 that they are generally given at God's initiative, rather than because people seek them.

Question 1. While the principal theme of this passage is prayer and spiritual warfare, Daniel's prayer involves a profound spiritual experience. It is important to ensure that in our Christian lives we do not seek spiritual experiences for their own sake. Our priority is to be more Christlike. The aim of this approach question is to put such experiences in context. Daniel's experience is incidental to the central meaning of the passage. This question may bring out a wide range of spiritual experiences, varying from those with definite experiences of the Holy Spirit (and who may be enthusiastic for others to enjoy the same) and those who are very suspicious of such events. Two distinctly opposing and usually strongly held views on this are either that "experiences" make you in some sense superior as a Christian, or that if you have such an experience, it is automatically suspect because it is merely "emotional." Try to encourage the group to assess how such experiences have changed or influenced their Christian lives and whether their experience(s) have actually increased their devotion to Christ and their Christlikeness—the test of an experience which is authentically of God. Bear in mind that many biblical characters experienced God in a variety of ways. We must not stereotype the way God deals with us on this level.

If you think it inappropriate to use this approach question with your group, an alternative question is "Describe how praying for a person or situation might change your understanding of the person or circumstances."

Question 2. Note verses 11-12 and 19 which underline his qualities and devotion. In spite of Daniel's remarkable faith and obedience (there is no recorded sin in the life of Daniel, although he was, of course, not sinless), the presence of the Lord rendered Daniel helpless (v. 8). (This reminds us also that the presence of God is far beyond our understanding, and would destroy us except for God's grace toward us.)

Question 3. If fasting is a new idea for the group, it is usually understood to mean going without food and drink for a certain period. Here Daniel gives up certain food and drink, presumably as a way of humbling himself, reflecting a state of mourning and asking for guidance from God.

Question 4. Daniel's previous angelic visitation (Daniel 9, around 539 B.C.) involved Gabriel explaining to him that the earthly opposition to his people would be overthrown. The purpose of the vision in 10:1—12:13 is positive assurance for God's people. Why God communicated as he did with Daniel we do not know for sure, but probably to demonstrate his strength and power so that Daniel (and those who would read of the vision in years to come) would be reassured. This may have been particularly necessary if the Jewish people believed their identity was going to be destroyed by exile in pagan Babylon. They may have come to doubt that God would work out his purposes for them. See verses 19, 21.

Question 5. Note the balance between God demonstrating his power and holiness—with which those present were humbled (vv. 7, 8, 15)—and the grace of God dealing gently with Daniel (vv. 10, 18) in his weakness. God understands our limitations and consequently protects us from things with which we cannot cope—even direct encounters with God himself which would be too much for us to withstand (see, for example, 1 Kings 19:11-13; Ex 33:20-23).

Question 6. Encourage the group to put themselves in Daniel's position. How would they have felt, and how might they have lived differently as a result of such an encounter with God?

Questions 7-8. This is a very difficult passage to interpret. The following should help you understand the general ideas behind the passage from which you are answering the questions:

☐ Parallel hierarchies of good and evil angelic beings exist in the spiritual realm (*New Bible Dictionary*, p. 358).

☐ Verse 12 indicates that God responded to Daniel's prayer and had come to him because of it.

☐ Unseen spiritual conflict lasted for three weeks (v. 13), which was the same length of time for which Daniel prays and mourns (vv. 2-3).

☐ The expression "the prince of the kingdom of Persia" represents a demonic being (a fallen angel) with a geographical or racial responsibility. Michael (10:21; 12:1) is, in contrast, the divine angel responsible for the Jews.

☐ Daniel is not fighting the battle directly—no human could. But Christ and the angelic servants of God are involved directly in the spiritual warfare. In prayer we can be caught up in these conflicts, which affect events in the world on a visible level. Ronald Wallace comments, "The heavenly host [angels] in their conflict need the support of earthly intercessors, and the earthly people of God in their conflict need the help of the heavenly host" (*The Message of Daniel*, pp. 178-79).

Question 9. Look at verses 12-14, 19, and 20-21 particularly. If you find the question difficult, start by listing things that God does in the passage and try to work out what the practical implications were for Daniel and his generation and have been for those who have read the story subsequently. Some clues are: God explains things to us (vv. 12, 14); God is active behind the scenes, although we may not see this (v. 13); God reassures us in the midst of conflict (v. 19); he tells us the truth (v. 21); he conquers evil (v. 21).

Questions 10-11. To know the mind of God we need to know the Bible and prayerfully apply its wisdom under the guidance of the Spirit to analyze and understand the world around us; and to pray obediently in accordance with our often limited understanding. Note however that Daniel is involved in the place of prayer (10:2) presumably without actually understanding what is going on. Often we will pray like this. But all the time we must pray for wisdom to know how to pray. If we do not understand why we pray as we do, we have to live with the fact that the significance of our prayers may only be understood after the event. As to what we are prompted to pray for, the Holy Spirit will never teach us anything inconsistent with Scripture, and any guidance or insight must always be weighed against the Bible's authoritative teaching to see if it is in line with Scripture's teaching.

Background reading: Ronald S. Wallace, *The Message of Daniel,* The Bible Speaks Today (Downers Grove, Ill.: InterVarsity Press, 1979). Joyce G. Baldwin, *Daniel,* Tyndale Old Testament Commentary (Leicester, U.K.: Inter-Varsity Press, 1978).

Study 5. Praying for the Nation. Ezekiel 22:23-31.

Purpose: To examine the significance of prayer and leadership in national life.

Background. Ezekiel would have been taken into exile with many of his people by the Babylonians around 597 B.C. He was called to be a prophet around 593 B.C., at a time when the people of God were surrounded by excessive idolatry and materialism in Babylon—a contrast to his upbringing in the temple as the child of a priest. (The studies on Daniel and Nehemiah provide more historical detail.)

You will note that while preparing the passage there are five "types" of leaders or groups described in the passage—depending on the Bible version(s) your group uses. To help deal with issues arising in the passage, the following notes may be helpful regarding each type of leader or group.

v. 25: *Princes* (NIV) refers to the members of the royal household; an alternative translation is *prophets* (NASB) (see also v. 28). There is debate by the commentators as to which is the correct translation. Using either does not significantly alter the general meaning of the passage.

v. 26: *Priests* were those who officiated in the temple and interceded for the people.

v. 27: *Officials* (NIV) or *princes* (NASB) refers to the politicians or ruling class/nobility.

v. 28: *Prophets* were those who claimed to speak for God (see note on v. 25).

v. 29: *People of the land* were those with full citizenship rights; they could oppress those without such rights; for example, aliens (immigrants) or slaves.

Question 1. Remember that there may be considerable differences of opinion between the group members as to whether Christians should have an active role in national life. If discussion becomes heated, postpone it until the end of the study.

Question 3. The aim of this question is to look at the effect of sin on the rest of society. (You may be able to discuss modern parallels in your own country, but try to avoid getting into a political argument!) Encourage the group to think through how the actions of one group or class affect other people. For example, does government corruption encourage ordinary people to be corrupt?

Question 4. The priests have deviated from the true faith in several ways (detailed in v. 26): breaking God's law, using things that were set apart for God (such as items in the temple) for pagan worship, lack of moral or theological discernment and blasphemy.

Question 5. The reference to prophets' "deeds" in verse 28 probably requires you to look back over the preceding verses to see which deeds are being "whitewashed" or disguised. Alternatively, they may be covering up their own misdeeds by claiming God's authority and inspiration for their actions, when he had not spoken through them.

It is important to distinguish between the New and Old Testament role of "prophet." In the Old Testament, the true prophet (such as Jeremiah) spoke verbally inspired infallible prophecy, with an objectivity which New Testament prophecy does not possess; the New Testament equivalent of the Old Testament prophets was the apostolic circle (Peter, Paul and so on) who laid down authoritative teaching on the faith (see Eph 2:20; 2 Pet 3:2). In the Old Testament the prophet was also personally called (see, for example, Ezek 2:3-7) by God, whereas his or her ministry in the New Testament is given by God and recognized by the church, and subject to its control and testing.

New Testament prophecy is constrained by its subjective and nonauthoritative nature. Paul felt free to disobey it (see Acts 21:4, 10-11 and 20:22) and certainly saw it as open to evaluation and testing (1 Cor 14:29-30). Also, comparisons of Acts 21:11 with Acts 21:32-33 show us that it may not be 100 percent accurate. While in the Old Testament any false prophet was stoned to death, in the New Testament the prophet was simply open to correction and evaluation (1 Cor 14:29-30), implying that prophecy in the New Testament is of a different nature than that in the Old Testament. It is not canonical, that is, part of the Bible, but is a continuing gift of insight that should be weighed against the Bible's authoritative teaching (1 Thess 5:19-21).

Question 7. These general questions, particularly the second, will be a useful indicator as to how well the group is beginning to understand intercession, particularly in the light of what it has learned in the previous studies.

Question 8. Some Christians believe all they can do is maintain their own spiritual lives and be fully involved in their churches. However, Christ's command in Matthew 5:13-16 to be salt and light calls us to be both a morally purifying influence in the world (salt) and a clear public witness (light). Much archaeological evidence indicates that the early church played a significant role in the public life of their communities. They prayed, evangelized and did good works, penetrating every aspect of their culture that was legitimate for a Christian to be involved in.

Question 9. Verse 30 only asks for a person to stand in the gap. A few can affect the many. It should also be borne in mind that in countries where there are many Christians, great idolatry and materialism can and does still exist!

Background reading: John B. Taylor, *Ezekiel,* Tyndale Old Testament Commentary (Downers Grove, Ill.: InterVarsity Press, 1969).

Study 6. Praying for Everyone. 1 Timothy 2:1-8.

Purpose: To explore the importance of prayer in the church, and to review the studies so far.

General Note. Questions 1, 4, 5, 7, 8 and 10 are "summary" questions, and you may want the group to look back at studies 1-5. Accordingly, this study may take a little longer than usual. So you will need to either (1) allocate more time for the study, or (2) ask people to look at the study in advance and answer the questions numbered above on their own, with a view to everyone sharing their answers when the group meets together (this will only work if everyone can have a copy of the study available to them), or (3) if the group is large enough, split into two or three groups and take two or three of the summary questions per group. Each smaller group can answer the questions and then share its answers with the rest of the group at the end of the meeting.

You may also want to have some summary ideas ready to offer to the group.

Question 3. Good doctrine (derived from good Bible knowledge and understanding) enables us to pray in accordance with God's will. (The previous studies underlined how much God's promises were used in biblical prayer.) Apart from showing no artificial division between truth and practice, Paul may be reminding his readers that God desires and commands evangelism, and they are to pray for all to learn of the good news of Christ. Note that verse 4 does not mean that everyone will become Christians; rather, God longs for all to come to accept what Christ has done for them, although many will not. (Because Western culture often finds accepting absolutes difficult, the clear statement by Paul in verse 5 that there is only one mediator between God and a man or woman may be considered unreasonable by some in the group. It is, however, clearly biblical.)

Question 5. Often we are very critical of non-Christians and look down on them, considering ourselves superior. The prayers of intercession studied so far show the intercessor caring for those under God's judgment, being willing even to perish that others might come to know Christ (see Paul's attitude in Romans 9:3).

Question 6. This is a difficult verse to interpret. Paul is probably implying that a socially peaceful environment (for example, where there is no civil war) is the best setting for the development of Christians' devotion, seriousness of purpose, attitude and character which is respected by nonbelievers. This does not mean to say, of course, that these qualities will not develop in other situations.

Question 9. Sin is a barrier to prayer (see, for example, Is 59:2; Jn 9:31). Disunity is a sign of sin, and unified prayer will not happen where Christians don't get together with each other. Lives also need to witness to Christ; if we teach about the love of Christ, the church must demonstrate it in its behavior.

Question 10. See how many of the following qualities the group tracks down:
- perseverance (Dan 10:3)
- responsiveness to God's prompting (Gen 18:23; Ex 32:11; Dan 10:2; Neh 1:4)
- repentance (Dan 10:2; Neh 1:6)
- willingness to take risks (Gen 18:30; Ex 32:10-11; Neh 1:11)
- courage (Gen 18:27; Ex 32:11; Neh 2:2-3)
- self-sacrifice (Dan 10:3)
- in-depth biblical knowledge and application (Gen 18:25; Ex 32:11; Neh 1:8-10)
- identity with sin of people (Neh 1:6)
- concern for God's glory and reputation (Gen 18:25)
- intimate relationship with God (Gen 18:22; Ex 32:1; Dan 10:2)
- humility before and fear of God (Gen 18:27, 32; Neh 1:5; Dan 10:12, 19)
- concern for others (Gen 18:11)
- integrity (Ezek 22:26; Dan 10:10)
- obedience to God's laws (Ezek 22:26)

☐ faithfulness to God's truth (Ezek 22:26)
☐ preparedness to take practical action (Neh 2:5; Ezek 22:30)
Question 12. See if you can discern how people's prayer lives have changed over the weeks you have been studying. You may find the group needs to be encouraged to be honest. It is important to understand that God's willingness to listen to our prayers does not depend on how impressive they sound. You may need to emphasize that growing in prayer is a lifelong discipline.

Background reading: Donald Guthrie, *The Pastoral Epistles,* Tyndale New Testament Commentary (Grand Rapids, Mich.: Eerdmans, 1957).

Study 7. Relying on God. Psalm 5.

Purpose: To examine how we should pray when under pressure.
Question 1. Often Christians become very discouraged when they face opposition or pressure, particularly if they are new to the Christian faith. These are times when we can learn about God and his faithfulness, rather than see opposition or pressure as a totally negative experience. Encourage the group to explore *why* they react as they do in these circumstances.
Question 3. Many people find praying at the start of the day very helpful—to get the day in perspective and pray when they are least tired. David in fact prayed both morning and evening (see Psalms 3—4). We need to be careful not to fall into legalism, in thinking that failing to pray, say, twice a day will make us less acceptable to God or that we can only pray at certain times of the day. On the other hand, it is a very useful model. A deep human relationship has communication with both short and instant and in-depth, deep conversations. Both are necessary in our relationship with God. Time deliberately set aside for solitary prayer is a crucial part of growing as a Christian.
Question 4. One example of what to look for is the way David addresses God (v. 2). David writes as a king—addressing a much greater one. David realizes that his acceptance by God is not based on his status, moral behavior or abilities. He can rely on God's mercy. See also verses 4, 7, 10 and 12.

Remember that the promise that God will shield us (v. 12) does not necessarily mean that we are never hurt or experience suffering; however, it will never be greater than we can bear, and it only happens with God's "permission." Our bodies and minds may suffer, but our relationship with God is secure.
Questions 7-8. Note references in the passage to (1) God's moral view of evil (v. 4), (2) God's practical opposition to evil (v. 10) and God's comfort of the believer (v. 11) during persecution.

Question 5. In distinguishing the two categories, the group might also observe that sometimes Christians demonstrate more characteristics of the wicked than of the righteous. We need to beware of hypocrisy. John teaches in 1 John that the mark of authentic Christian belief is not only correct doctrine but a life consistent with it.

Question 6. We can be confident of both the sovereignty of God over those who do evil and the ultimate justice of God in dealing with them. We know the evildoers will receive a just reward for their wrongdoing, even if evil appears to succeed now in a human sense.

One point which might be useful in helping us to understand the source of evil is the fact that if God is perfect and he can do no wrong, then he is sinless. This does not mean, however, that God does not "regret" things happening; for example, he "regrets" that we ever rebelled against him, but it is not his fault. God is sovereign over and responsible for the universe, but he cannot be blamed for its sin and evil.

Background reading: Derek Kidner, *Psalms 1-72,* Tyndale Old Testament Commentary (Downers Grove, Ill.: InterVarsity Press, 1973).

Study 8. Being Honest with God. 1 Samuel 1.

Purpose: To understand that God is both interested in and responds to prayers about our personal circumstances and needs, and how he uses the suffering of an individual to bring about his wider purposes.

Background. This story is set around 1100-1050 B.C., at the end of the period during which Israel was ruled by "judges." The nation was in considerable moral and spiritual decline. Out of the human need and difficulty of a family situation, God brought into being Samuel, who became a judge of Israel, a prophet and the one who anointed its first king.

Don't read any significance into the fact that both the prayers of women in this LifeGuide are connected with the subject of children. The Bible has more prayers by women than most people imagine. The book of Esther and the song of Deborah (Judg 5) are omissions I regret; they are omitted simply because they did not cover the subject material under consideration here.

Question 1. Some Christians find it very hard to believe that suffering can in any way be positive, especially during the suffering itself. Try not to let the discussion drift into a general discussion of suffering.

Question 2. Verse 3 seems to indicate consistent worship, in comparison to the priests of the day who were leading scandalous lives (1 Sam 2:12-17). Someone in the group may pick up on the fact that Elkanah had two wives, and see this as inconsistent with godly living. (Abraham, too, had concubines and secondary wives such as Hagar.) While this was recognized as legal in Deuteronomy (presumably as a concession to cultural pressures), it was originally recognized in Genesis that one wife (monogamy) was the norm, and this is reflected throughout the Scriptures. God still appears to recognize Elkanah and Hannah as godly people, despite this deviation from biblical standards. It appears that God chose, in this instance, to bring about his purposes through believing parents and that Elkanah and Hannah were appropriate people to parent Samuel.

Question 4. Discussion may be helped by the group putting themselves in Hannah's situation and trying to imagine the conflicts she might have felt. Does she want a child to please herself, to please Elkanah, to please God or to spite Peninnah? Hannah clearly suffers greatly in her infertility, such that she cannot be comforted (v. 8). It would be reasonable to assume that she feels great conflicts about her desire for a child. Yet she does not block her communication with God by allowing bitterness or resentment to mar her relationship with him, which we can easily do.

Some members of the group may worry that they are unable to pray to God unless they have entirely pure motives. Our thought life will be no more perfect than the rest of our life while we continue to live in mortal bodies. While we cannot be sinless this side of heaven, the key test is whether we aspire to be like Christ and long to be holy. Despite the highest motives, we live with the reality that even if we desire and work to discover God's will in our hearts and minds, our motives will not be absolutely pure. Remind the group that Jesus himself experienced conflict in prayer between his will and God's will (yet, of course, without sin; see Lk 22:42). One of the most important ways of dealing with impure motives or reasons for praying is to confess them to God, asking him to forgive and to change us. Useful further references on this issue include James 1:5; 1 John 5:14-15; Romans 8:26-27 and Luke 18:9-14.

Question 5. Hannah may not at the time have understood her prayer to have been prompted by God, but verse 5 makes it clear that her childlessness was because of the Lord's action. She prayed because she was childless, so her prayer was ultimately prompted by God.

Question 6. Many factors can limit our honesty with God. We may think he is not interested, we may be frightened of him or we may have been criticized as a child for demonstrating emotion and, consequently, project our false perceptions onto God. Try to encourage the group to think through how their fears or inhibitions line up in the light of what we know about the character of God in the Bible.

Question 8. Look particularly at verse 11, 22 and verses 25-28. Like anything God gives us, Hannah's son was not hers for selfish pleasure, but a gift from God which was to be offered in the service of God. The reference to the vow in verse 11 implies that she saw the child as "separated" or "consecrated" for God, which would be symbolized in Hannah's culture by his hair not being cut. A similar concept is referred to in Numbers 6 and Judges 13:5. Hannah's faithfulness to God was later rewarded (see 1 Sam 2:18-21).

A parallel even concerning a parent giving up their child to God is recorded in the story of Abraham in Genesis 22.

Question 9. John White comments: "The same pain that produced a Samuel to transform Israel, produced a transformed Hannah. If we could have talked with her ten years after the birth of Samuel (long before Samuel became a national figure) we would have found that she had never ceased to sound the praises of the God who had "tormented" her. She would laugh at the pain. Laugh at it not only because God had answered her but because pain had driven her into the arms of God. . . . Hannah was not a pawn in God's historical chess game. God's purposes for Hannah might have involved pain. But his larger purpose for Israel was linked with a loving purpose for Hannah" (John White, *Daring,* pp. 88-89).

Question 10. A number of factors may have affected her; for example, the encouragement and blessing of Eli, who had initially misinterpreted her; the relief of being able to explain her feelings to God; a subjective sense of assurance after having prayed; and possibly her past experience of answered prayer giving her confidence that God had "heard" her. She addresses the Lord as the "LORD Almighty" in verse 11, a term which carries the meaning of God being seen as infinite and all powerful.

Question 11. Their behavior, by taking Samuel to the temple, was consistent with what Hannah had promised they would do; she played a part in fulfilling her own prayer request; the boy would be consecrated to God.

Question 13. 1 Samuel 2:1-10 is a song expressing Hannah's confidence and trust in the God whom she worshiped and who had answered her prayer. Even having given her son back to God after waiting so long for him, she could praise God. The two passages should give the group some things for which they can thank God. Try to spend at least five minutes in silence as a group, reading and reflecting on the passage in chapter 2 before sharing what has been learned from it and from the group study.

Background reading: John White, *Daring,* chapter 6. Joyce Baldwin, *1 and 2 Samuel,* Tyndale Old Testament Commentary (Downers Grove, Ill.: Inter-Varsity Press, 1988).

Study 9. Thanking God. Luke 1:46-55.

Purpose: To study the importance of thanking God and its place in our prayer life.

Question 1. Some of the group may have difficult personal circumstances (for example, a broken marriage, poverty or suffering). They may find it embarrassing to be honest in a group situation.

Question 2. The view we have of God will shape the way we see ourselves and how we talk to God. Mary refers particularly to three aspects of his character—his holiness (v. 49), his power (v. 52) and his mercy (v. 54).

Question 4. In verses 46-47, do not read any significance into the technical difference between "soul" and "spirit." The use of the different words owes more to the structure of the poetry in the original language than to any intended difference of meaning or function.

You may need to explain the meaning of the words *glorify* and *rejoice* to be able to get the most out of the question. For the Christian to glorify the Lord involves giving praise to God for his actions and who he is—to honor and respect him. This will be both verbally and by our attitudes and actions. Rejoicing involves praising and expressing our thanks to God. It would be a useful exercise when preparing this study to look up other uses of the two words in the Bible using a concordance. If time permits, encourage the group to think about not just the words they use but also their attitudes. We can say thank you without really meaning it!

Question 5. You may find the group confused about the meaning of fear. We often interpret it as in a horror movie—fear means terror. While we can be rightly terrified of God and his judgment because of our sin, knowledge of the love of God in Christ should cast out that type of fear for anyone who relies on what Jesus did on the cross to make them right with God. A biblical fear of God is based on respect and reverence, not terror. Christians can be very flippant and sloppy in their view of God, forgetting that he is the great and all-powerful God. We can also be wrongly frightened of him because we do not understand his love and mercy. It is important for us to fear God in the right sense in order to pray with the correct attitude. Sometimes we pray as if God is our servant. We try to order him around. The other extreme is to be so frightened of him that we do not approach him and are too frightened to ask him anything. You may find both of these extremes in the group. A right fear of God is positive, not negative, and leads to his mercy and blessing being known and experienced.

Question 6. Often our prayers concentrate on our personal spiritual experience and lack a breadth of vision of what God has done and is doing. Mary could have only prayed about the Christ she was to bear (and she does in vv. 48-49). But she also thanks God for a whole range of other things that he has done in vv. 50-55. She is not narrow minded, so her prayer is richer. The broader our understanding of the Bible, the wider the range of things about which we can pray and give thanks. So our prayer life is enriched.

Question 7. See also question 6. Helping the friend to look outside of their situation and needs to see what God has done should help them to get their own circumstances in perspective. To see how God has worked in history helps us to see how he can and will work in the situations we face.

Question 8. It is easy for us as Christians to harbor attitudes which God has condemned in the nonbeliever, for example, pride, arrogance and self-satisfied preoccupation with wealth. Sin in our lives will undermine our prayer lives. Pride, arrogance and preoccupation with wealth/status/power can render us unable to thank God, appreciate him or serve him. What Mary describes is both a warning and at the same time an encouragement to us. God reigns supreme over human greed and wrongdoing.

Question 9. Often we underuse the Bible in our times of prayer. Mary's knowledge of how God had fulfilled his promises enabled her to thank God for what he had done.

Question 10. This question is designed to help the group think about how balanced their prayer lives are. Some Christians spend all their time telling God how wonderful he is, but never intercede for others. Some always pray for others but never thank God or pray for themselves. Our prayer lives need to reflect the biblical balance of prayer. There are many types of prayer—including intercession, thanksgiving, praise, repentance, asking for forgiveness, listening to God, bringing God our personal needs. There also needs to be balance as to for whom and what we pray.

Background reading: Leon Morris, *Luke,* Tyndale New Testament Commentary (Grand Rapids, Mich.: Eerdmans, 1974).

Study 10. Blessing Other People. Ephesians 1:15-23 and 3:14-21.

Purpose: To explore how Paul's prayer for Christians is a model for our prayer.

Background. This letter was probably written for a wider group of Christians than the church at Ephesus, and circulated around several churches in Asia Minor. Paul's priorities seem to have been (1) to reassure believers who they were in Christ, (2) to remind them what was available to them in Christ, and (3) to instruct them how they should live together despite their different backgrounds.

The book contains two prayers, and the two passages we look at give us an understanding of how Paul prayed for the Christians he knew.

Question 1. This is designed to get the group thinking about what they want most for people. Is our highest desire for non-Christians that they see Christ and turn to him? And for Christians that they become more like Christ? If so, how do we pray toward these goals?

Question 3. If the group finds this a difficult exercise, the following structure may help to give you a basis to start from.

1:15-16. Paul gives thanks for their faith.

1:17-19a. Paul prays that the believers might fully experience what God has done for them.

1:19b-23. Paul focuses on God's power.

3:16-17a. Paul prays for the strengthening of the believers.

3:17b-19. Paul concentrates on the limitless love of God.

Question 4. Under the inspiration of the Holy Spirit, Paul's prayer arises out of the truths expressed in 1:3-14. Get the group to read 1:3-14, but make sure you concentrate on how Paul's prayer flows out of the truths in it. Don't get sidetracked into discussing 1:3-14 itself. Using the Bible helps us to ensure our prayer is in line with God's will, and enables God to speak to us and guide/correct us as we pray.

> Prayer is a fire which needs fuel to burn and a match light it. If the fire burns low, we can fan it so that the flame may burn more fiercely. But all the fanning in the world cannot create a bonfire from a single match nor from a pile of dead cold fuel.
>
> Fire must come from above; indeed it has already come. The Holy Spirit burns quietly within the Christian ready to light the fuel of Scripture's truth. But the fuel must be there. (John White, *Daring,* p. 126.)

Paul grounds his prayer in biblical truth about Christ, specifically God's choice of us to know him ("election") in 1:4-6, the fact that now we experience God's adoption of us into his family (1:5-8) and the future blessing of being one with God (1:9-10). Finally, Paul underlines how these blessings are true for each believer, Jew or Gentile, in 1:11-13.

Question 5. Paul reminds us in 2 Corinthians 5:16 that we can no longer look at people from a worldly point of view; we must see those around us as Christ does and serve them accordingly. It is easy to assume that Christ feels the same about people as we do; instead, we should increasingly feel about them as he does.

Question 6. Encourage the group to put themselves in the position of the people Paul prayed for, and see if they can imagine what would have happened to them when Paul's prayers were answered.

For the second part of the question, it might help to get the group to rewrite this part of Paul's prayer as if he prayed it for non-Christians.

Question 7. Paul emphasizes the death and resurrection of Christ as the cornerstone of the Christian faith. Paul wants them to be fully identified with Christ so that the power of the cross is being worked out daily in their lives.

Question 8. Note the parallel themes of understanding (for example, 1:17-18) and intimate depth of relationship (for example, 3:16-19) in the two prayers. Being a Christian was not just about correct doctrine but also about being in a relationship with God in Christ. Francis Foulkes comments, "Paul was aware of a danger, especially in the churches of the Greek world, of a faith that depended simply on intellectual knowledge" (*Ephesians,* Tyndale New Testament Commentary [Grand Rapids, Mich.: Eerdmans, 1989], p. 112).

Question 9. This question may reveal limitations in some group members' understanding of the love of Christ for them, and for others; often people find it hard to accept that Christ loves them personally. They may understand the idea that he loves them but not be conscious of it. The balance is to be both assured of the truth and to experience it. Remember that just because someone cannot feel Christ's love, that does not mean that Christ does not love them. You may need to defer discussion of this until after the main part of the study is over, if it is clear that a lot of issues need to be discussed.

Question 10. Often we lose sight of the fact that God can change situations and people that we see as unchangeable. Realism is important so that we don't have false expectations. But hope inspires us to see God as bigger than the "problems."

Question 11. Two issues will probably arise here: the attitudes we have toward other people that we pray for, and the way our prayer might now change in the light of the teaching on prayer the group has received—whether from this study or more generally.

Question 12. You may wish to devote some prayer time at the end of the study to pray for others more biblically. This may involve some confession of wrong attitudes.

Background Reading: John White, *Daring,* chapter 9. John R. W. Stott, *The Message of Ephesians* (Downers Grove, Ill.: InterVarsity Press, 1979). D. A. Carson, *A Call to Spiritual Reformation* (Grand Rapids, Mich.: Baker, 1992), chapters 10 and 11. Francis Foulkes, *Ephesians.*

Study 11. Praying Together. Acts 4:23-31.

Purpose: To learn about unity in group prayer, the importance of understanding God's control over circumstances and how to pray when facing opposition.

Background. The setting for the passage is Acts 3:1—4:22. Peter and John have been used by God to heal a cripple, and they then speak about Christ. The temple authorities imprison them overnight and try to stop them teaching about Christ. Their response is, "We cannot help speaking about what we have seen and heard" (4:20). They are then released and return to their friends.

Question 1. This discussion may reveal a number of different attitudes and experiences—some positive, some negative. Note carefully any issues raised and note any help or further discussion that might be needed. If the group members relate sufficiently well to each other, the practical exercise at the end of the study could be a helpful way of developing the group's prayer life together.

Question 3. It is not clear from the passage precisely how the group prayed together; it would be difficult for them to pray together an identical prayer without having planned it first. It may have been that they prayed sentence by sentence following someone who led the prayer, or that the prayer recorded is a summary. Regardless of the way they prayed together, the critical point is that they prayed from the strength of their unity. See also Acts 4:32.

The quotation in verses 25-26 is from Psalm 2.

Question 4. It's particularly difficult to be dishonest in open prayer to God; to pray together demands genuine unity. It also cements the aims of the group if they all pray together toward the same objectives.

Question 6. The central issue is God's sovereignty (or ultimate control) over circumstances. This is illustrated by the Psalm 2 quotation, clearly identifying that God's purposes are not defeated by the political, military or legal powers of governments opposed to his purposes. Indeed, God even used the unlawful crucifixion of Christ to bring about his purposes in history, namely, saving us. It should be borne in mind, however, that the historical actions of Herod (for example) were not forced upon him—he chose to act as he did. God works out his plan in history without robbing men and women of their freedom. The fact that the early church could see their persecution as potentially bringing about God's purposes meant they did not see persecution as an overwhelming threat. This must have affected their attitudes toward those who persecuted them—just as Christ prayed, "Father, forgive them, for they do not know what they are doing" (Lk 23:34).

Question 7. The believers clearly did not lose sight of the overall mission God had for them; interestingly, they do not pray for their personal protection, but instead for boldness.

Question 8. Often we are surprised when God answers prayer because in reality we lacked the faith to believe he would. Here the dramatic way God answered was presumably an indication of his power, to reassure the church. An earthquake was often understood in the Old Testament as an indicator of God's presence (Ex 19:18; Is 6:4).

Question 9. Our desire for an experience of the Holy Spirit can be selfish, rather than seeking to be better equipped to serve God and witness to Christ. (Naturally, we should constantly seek a deeper walk with God through the Holy Spirit's work, but not just to satisfy our own sense of spiritual well-being.) The expression "filled with the Holy Spirit" may generate a debate as to what this means and why it occurs, and whether we should seek such experiences. Try to avoid getting into a complex discussion on this point. Whatever the experience of the believers in this situation, the net effect was a new empowering for evangelism. This ties in precisely with the words of Jesus in Acts 1:8, "But you will receive power when the Holy Spirit comes on you; and you will be my witnesses in Jerusalem, and in all Judea and Samaria, and to the ends of the earth." In experience-oriented cultures we often look to God as a source of constant personal spiritual experience and gratification, rather than seeing his gift of the Spirit as the one who makes us Christlike and enables us to fulfill his commission in the world.

Questions 10-11. To deal with problems highlighted in question 10, the group will have to be very practical and possibly firm with itself as to how it prays together in order to make the less-confident group members feel at ease. Both in discussing praying together and in evangelism, some less confident members of the group may be fearful of both activities. They may be frightened off or made to feel guilty by the more confident members of the group. Be sensitive to their problems here, and the need to encourage them. Bear in mind also that evangelism is not just verbally explaining the gospel; for some in the group the most effective way they can witness might be to take a Christian ethical stance in the work environment. Words and deeds must run hand in hand in evangelism.

   Background reading: I. Howard Marshall, *Acts,* Tyndale New Testament Commentary (Grand Rapids, Mich.: Eerdmans, 1980). John R. W. Stott, *The Message of Acts* (Downers Grove, Ill.: InterVarsity Press, 1990).

Study 12. Praying with Confidence. Luke 11:1-13.

Purpose: (1) To understand Jesus' instruction to us as to how we should pray, (2) to explore God's attitudes toward us and our prayers as described in some of the parables of Jesus, (3) to develop our understanding about persistence in prayer, (4) to learn about the way God answers prayer, and (5) to learn more about his character.

Background. This section of Jesus' teaching on prayer arises out of his disciples' request for teaching (11:1). Verses 2-4 include what most Christian traditions call "The Lord's Prayer," which is also found in Matthew 6:9-13 in a slightly longer form. As Jesus intended the prayer as a pattern, not a rigid formula, it is not surprising that he taught it more than once. This also explains the variation in wording.

General Note. Questions 8-10 are designed to be more general summary questions looking back over the studies in this LifeGuide. You may need to lead the group study in a different way—see the general note in the leader's notes for study 6—to get the most out of the study questions.

Question 1. Hopefully, some of the points on which your group needs reassurance will be covered during the study. Note the issues raised, and review during the practical exercise what has been covered and what is still outstanding.

Remember that Christians' difficulties with prayer are sometimes symptoms of problems in their relationship with God. If we have a wrong view of God, we may doubt (for example) that he hears our prayers or wants to answer them. Apart from Jesus' example to his disciples as to how to pray, he gave his followers practical teaching about prayer. Just as he taught about the character of God, he demonstrated the character of God in his life on earth to help us to understand and approach him. He wants us to have confidence in approaching God, but not arrogance. We cannot order God around.

Question 2. The following is a brief analysis of the key points in the Lord's prayer which should help the group if the pattern within it is not immediately obvious.

(1) "Father" implies intimacy with God, as a child would address his parent, enabling us to understand that we can talk to God with intimacy. Despite who he is, he is approachable and sees us as his children.

(2) "Hallowed" (NIV) means "made holy"; the phrase "Hallowed be your name" means we should approach God with reverence, aware of his nature and character.

(3) "Your kingdom come" has two aspects to it: in the present those who pray should long to see Christ's rule realized in the lives of men and women, and also long for the future reality that Christ will finally come and ensure that his will is perfectly done everywhere.

(4) The prayer then moves in verse 3 from a focus on God's character and the outworking of his purposes to a prayer for the provision of our daily needs ("daily bread"), emphasizing our continual dependence on God. This discourages us from being arrogantly self-reliant or forgetful of his constant provision.

(5) The final part of the prayer (v. 4) demonstrates that we can confidently approach a merciful God for forgiveness, and in being forgiven find the grace of God to forgive others.

The closing request, "And lead us not into temptation" (NIV), does not mean that we ask God not to tempt us, for he does not tempt us to sin (see Jas 1:13). Instead it implies that in our weakness we come to God, recognizing the temptations around us, to ask that we might be able to resist the temptations we face and so lead a holy life.

The framework this provides for us involves therefore intimacy, reverence, a longing for the outworking of God's purposes, dependence on God and desiring to live a holy life, resisting temptation in God's strength. The group's familiarity with the Lord's Prayer may mean they have not looked at it in detail.

Question 3. To provide food and hospitality to a visitor was expected practice in Jesus' culture. The friend probably lived in a one-room house, so to get up to provide the bread would have awakened the family. Because the first friend persists in asking, thereby demonstrating the seriousness of his need for bread, his request is answered.

Question 4. The concept of "answers" to prayer is complicated. The following will give you a framework for discussion if the group is unable to clearly draw out ideas from the passage.

As with the parable of the widow in Luke 18, God is not being likened to a grudging friend, an unkind father or an unjust judge in the way that he answers our prayers. The parable says, "If a human is like this, think how much more kind God is."

God responds to prayer not because he has to be pushed into it, but because he wants to give to us and to use us in accordance with his will (see v. 13 and 1 Jn 5:14). The reference in verse 13 to the Holy Spirit implies that the gift of the Holy Spirit to us is God's "best" for us, because he is the one who makes real to us what Christ has done for us. It is doubtful that Luke has used the expression here to refer to the dispensing of particular charismatic gifts.

If the answer to our prayer is not as we expect, it is always a sufficient answer (see v. 8). We get what we need, not always what we want! And an answer must be within God's will. However, from a human level some answers may not seem the best—or even desirable. But God, as a totally just and righteous God, will ultimately work out things in accordance with his plan. As hard as we try, we cannot "blame" God in the sense that he is morally wrong to act in a particular way. God cannot sin. Because we do not understand why God does something does not mean that he is wrong.

Often we want answers to our prayers which satisfy us, rather than answers in line with God's will. We also have to bear in mind that the way God works never limits human free will. We may pray for a friend to become a Christian (and we should), but God cannot force them to do so.

Verses 11-13 point out by implication that if we view God as an unkind father (rather than a perfect one) we will be frightened to ask him, so we will never receive. Our faith is therefore undermined by wrong attitudes. We don't receive because we never ask.

Question 5. Note that the words *ask, seek* and *knock* are continuous tenses, that is, they imply constant "asking," "seeking" and "knocking." Also, the three words imply degrees of intensity. First you ask, then you seek, then you knock. The underlying issue is similar to that in verses 5-8; if we really seek God's will and want to see our prayer answered in line with his will, we should constantly pray. On these verses Leon Morris comments: "Jesus does not say and does not mean that, if we pray, we shall always get exactly what we ask for. After all, 'No' is just as definite an answer as 'Yes'. He is saying that true prayer is neither unheard nor unheeded. It is always answered in the way God sees is best" (*Luke,* p. 196).

Question 6. We have seen from other studies (for example, study 4 on Daniel 10) that prayer often involves spiritual warfare. Because of the importance of prayer in our relationship with God, Satan will do his best to undermine individual and group prayer. The question presents an opportunity to encourage members of the group to do practical things to help each other pray, for example, meeting one-to-one with another group member to pray regularly.

Question 7. An alternative discussion question might be "How has this study changed your view of God?" This should help the group reflect on the character of God portrayed in the passage.

Question 8. This question is designed to help the group reflect on the variety of prayer.

Question 9. This question should draw out whether we are praying in a selfish or imbalanced way. Given the importance of evangelism, intercession should be a dominant part of our prayer lives. You can explore both the different sorts of prayer highlighted in the studies and the issues raised in question 2 of this study.

Question 10. This may be a difficult question for the group to relate to if they cannot identify obvious spiritual opposition. However, growth in Christian devotion and witness amongst any group of Christians is usually met with resistance at some point.

Question 11. Try to make this as practical as possible. Don't let the group set itself unrealistic goals. It's bettter to achieve several modest goals than fail to achieve an impossible one. It may be that group members need to meet in twos or threes to pray for other people—and each other—over the next few weeks; or for the whole group to meet (say over breakfast) to have more time to pray together.

Background reading: Leon Morris, *Luke*.

David Healey is a former student executive member and staffworker of UCCF, the British and Irish evangelical student movement. He lives in Sutton Coldfield near Birmingham in England and speaks regularly to student groups on the Christian faith, as well as working in marketing. He enjoys travel and photography.